N E W   C R A F T S

Appliqué

NEW CRAFTS

APPLIQUÉ

25 inspirational sewing projects shown step by step

PETRA BOASE

Photography by Polly Wreford

LORENZ BOOKS

This edition is published by Lorenz Books,
an imprint of Anness Publishing Ltd,
Great Russell Street
London WC1B 3NA

info@anness.com

www.lorenzbooks.com;
www.annesspublishing.com

If you like the images in this book and would
like to investigate using them for publishing,
promotions or advertising, please visit our website
www.practicalpictures.com for more information.

Publisher: Joanna Lorenz
Senior Editor: Lindsay Porter
Designers: Lilian Lindblom and Lucy Doncaster
Step photographer: Mark Wood
Stylist: Leeann Mackenzie
Illustrator: Madeleine David and Vana Haggerty

© Anness Publishing Ltd 2013

PUBLISHER'S NOTE
Although the advice and information in this book are believed to be
accurate and true at the time of going to press, neither the authors
nor the publisher can accept any legal responsibility or liability for
any errors or omissions that may have been made nor for any
inaccuracies nor for any loss, harm or injury that comes about from
following instructions or advice in this book.

Bracketed terms are intended for American readers.

PICTURE CREDITS
The author and publishers would like to thank the following for
additional photography: by courtesy of the board of trustees of the
Victoria and Albert Museum, pages 8 and 9; Patrick Gorman, page
10 and Joseph Ortenzi, page 17

CONTRIBUTORS
The author and publishers would like to thank the following for
their designs:
Victoria Brown: Christmas Tree Stars, Felt Curtain and Angelic
Babygrow; Lucinda Ganderton: Hands and Hearts Throw, Country
Candleshades, Broderie Perse Tablecloth, Ribbon Cushion and Lace
Cushion; Jo Gordon: Heart-warming Hats; Isabel Stanley: Mosaic
Velvet Cushion; Daniella Zimmerman: Organza Evening Bag, Rose
Petal Lampshade and Felted Appliqué Organza.

CONTENTS

INTRODUCTION

Appliqué is an extremely versatile method of applying and securing different pieces of fabric on to a background, which is then enriched by decorative stitches. Appliqué has been practised all over the world for centuries, with many different styles and techniques developing. There are no limitations to the methods of appliqué: it can be bold and colourful, pictorial or abstract, and both simple and complex designs can be created. The 25 diverse and exciting projects in this book are examples of different methods of appliqué using an assortment of interesting fabrics and decorative trimmings and stitches to create inspiring items for you to make.

Opposite: Simple shapes in ice-cream colours are used to great effect in these appliqué designs, illustrating that strikingly contemporary pieces can be created from an age-old technique.

HISTORY OF APPLIQUÉ

Appliqué has been practised for centuries by most cultures throughout the world. Its origins were initially practical: scraps of cloth could be re-used by sewing them to background fabrics, prolonging the life of clothing and materials that may have been scarce. It is interesting to trace how these concerns inspired a means of creative expression; the fabrics could be cut into shapes and embellished with stitching. As different techniques developed independently throughout the world, varying styles emerged.

Although appliqué developed very simply as a method of repairing worn items of clothing, examples have been found dating back as far as 980BC when animal hides were used by the ancient Egyptians to embellish funeral tents.

During the Middle Ages, appliqué became a very fashionable and functional method of working for needleworkers: because of its relatively low cost, it became a very strong substitute for the more costly and time-consuming solid embroidery. Fabrics were applied to items as diverse as household furnishings, heraldic flags and costumes. Appliqué was especially popular on ecclesiastical robes and altar frontals. In these instances linen shapes were cut out and applied to a velvet or silk background with an edging of cord or silk strands. The appliquéd shapes would then be embellished with rich gold stitching.

During the Renaissance, appliqué became a lavish form of embellishment on furnishings and hangings throughout the palaces and castles of the upper classes and royalty. As well as being exquisitely executed and beautifully decorated, many of the appliquéd hangings were hung and draped around the home for warmth, especially in doorways and around four-poster beds to shut out draughts.

In peasant cultures, the appliqué tradition was equally strong: precious remnants of more costly fabrics such as silk would be cut into shapes and appliquéd on to damaged parts of clothing or applied to domestic articles. This grew from economic necessity, but it also created many sophisticated results. Thus appliqué became strongly associated with folk art, and evidence of the technique appears in most cultures throughout the world. In Hungary, leather appliqué became very popular among

Above: Appliqué examples have been found dating back centuries, and practical motives, such as repairing worn cloth, soon gave way to decorative effects. This leather tunic dates from 6–7th century AD. The appliqué inserts are made from woven tapestry.

peasant societies and was very much a status symbol because of the expense of the fabric involved.

Throughout the United States, appliqué developed independently through quilt designs. Patterns were handed down from generation to generation and were often based on natural imagery such as birds, baskets, fruit, bouquets of flowers and garlands. Economy made the quilt popular throughout America as each scrap of fabric left over from cutting clothing was saved, and quilts were an essential part of the home for practical reasons because of the austere winters. Some quilts had so much work put into them that they were often kept for privileged guests or for display in the home.

Many of the techniques that inspire contemporary work draw on the intricate and unusual methods practised throughout South East Asia and India. In India, appliqué was commonly used to make religious hangings for festivals and ceremonies. The fabrics chosen would often depend on the importance of the event. The images portrayed in the designs were often drawn from mythology and were very spiritually symbolic. In South East Asia, intricate maze patterns were created using a cut-work method. The designs were highly intricate and were used in the decoration of clothing and hangings. In many tribes the skill is still a central part of women's work.

The 20th and 21st centuries brought exciting and innovative design movements. Today, appliqué is rich and varied in style and is used for different applications. Many of the methods used are drawn from traditional techniques practised through history all over the world. Machine-stitching has become a very popular method of applying and

embellishing appliqué shapes and there are now many forms of fabric bondings and adhesives on the market to aid faster methods of appliqué. Appliqué is often seen as the fabric equivalent of paper collage and should be executed in a similarly spontaneous way.

With the diverse choice of fabrics and embellishments available, artists can make their designs as individual and innovative as they desire.

Above: A beautiful example of a decorative panel dating from 19th-century Persia. Brightly coloured woollen cloth pieces were applied to a main background fabric and embellished with decorative embroidery stitches, including chain stitch. This exquisite example of the needleworker's art combines many of the most appealing aspects of appliqué.

GALLERY

Designers use appliqué to create an outstanding range of objects and effects. The pieces on the following pages start with the same basic technique but the results are as diverse as their creators. The following examples use materials from paper to plastic and all manner of natural fabrics. They make a good starting point for personal creations.

Right: NOUGHTS AND CROSSES This embroidered wall hanging is made in nine sections using a combination of hand- and machine-stitching to appliqué silk, cotton, chiffon and velvet on to a background fabric. Charlotte Hodge

Left: SPOT
LAMPSHADE
*A fabric-covered shade is
embellished with buttons
and bright circles of colour
using the cut-work
technique. The appliqué
shapes are sewn behind the
background fabric which is
then cut away to reveal the
new colours beneath.
Helen Rawlinson*

Above: SHOWER
CURTAIN
*Brightly coloured PVC
(vinyl) fabric and bold
designs are used to great
effect in this eye-catching
shower curtain.
Anne Delauney*

Far right and right:
PAPER APPLIQUÉ
HANGING AND
DETAIL
The combination of
materials and subtle
tones makes this piece
very striking. Hand-
made paper squares
are stitched on to a
background fabric.
Small squares of
hand-painted muslin
(cheesecloth) form the
central motif.
Christine Smith

Left: WALL
HANGING
The artist uses
photographic images
transferred on to
fabric, which are then
appliquéd on to a
background fabric.
Natasha Kerr

Opposite: BEADED
APPLIQUE
FLOWER
Beads add texture
and detail to this
simple, stylized flower
decoration for a loose
chair cover. In a
design of strong
shapes and colour
contrasts, created in
sturdy fabrics, their
delicacy creates a
delightful surprise.
Petra Boase

Right: SHADOW-
APPLIQUÉ
WAISTCOAT
*Natural linen forms the
basis of this waistcoat,
made special by the
appliqué designs on
the pockets. The pattern
pieces were cut from
scraps of coloured silk,
machine-stitched in
place, then covered with
a layer of organza.*
Louise Brownlow

Right: CHILD'S
CARDIGAN
*Felt patchwork pieces
in harlequin colours are
decorated with simple
felt shapes held in place
with contrasting
coloured threads.
Blanket stitch finishes
off the cuffs and hems.*
Katie Mawson

Above: WALL
HANGING
*Architectural shapes
are used in an almost
abstract manner in
this appliquéd and
machine-embroidered
wall hanging.*
Charlotte Hodge

Left: EGYPTIAN
APPLIQUE
Two vibrantly
opposed colours are
used for this Egyptian
appliqué, which
draws its imagery
from Islamic art. The
design has been cut
from several pieces of
blue cotton, appliquéd
onto a contrasting
pink background
cloth.
Lucinda Ganderton

Above: SPONGE
BAG

The perfect accessory
for the designer's
shower curtain, the
basic shape was made
using a patchwork
technique, then
decorated with quirky
designs held in place
with running stitch.
Anne Delauney

MATERIALS

Your own choice of fabrics, trimmings and embellishments is what makes a piece of appliqué work personal and unique. Select fabrics carefully and collect as many as possible to choose from. Look out for remnants at reduced prices and never throw left-over scraps of fabric away – you will find a use for them one day. There are many other materials that you may find useful for appliqué, a selection is listed below.

Beads and buttons These are both available in a wide range of colours, materials, sizes and shapes. Use buttons for decoration as well as fastenings, and to fasten quilts. Do not use buttons or beads on children's projects as they could come off and pose a choking hazard.

Binding tape This can be used for finishing edges.

Craft adhesive spray This is a spray-on glue that should be used sparingly and in a well-ventilated area. It is useful for fixing fabric on to thin card (stock).

Double-sided adhesive tape This is used to stick fabric on to thin card or paper. It is not as strong as adhesive spray, so the pieces may not last as long.

Embroidery threads (floss) These are available in many different thicknesses and textures. Stranded cotton threads can be separated; use two strands for fine work. Use embroidery threads to decorate or to secure fabrics.

Fabric glue This can be used instead of iron-on fusible bonding web to secure fabrics or trimmings together. It should be applied sparingly.

Fabrics Many kinds of fabric can be used in appliqué and you will often be able to use up remnants and other scraps. See the individual projects for advice on which fabrics are suitable for which technique or end use. Fabrics such as cotton can be dyed to obtain the desired colour for a particular design.

Felt Because this is a non-woven fabric, felt is easy to cut and does not fray, making it very suitable for appliqué.

Iron-on fusible bonding web This is a very effective material for fixing two pieces of fabric together. It consists of a fine web of adhesive, which is activated by the heat of an iron (see Basic Techniques). The result is washable and very durable.

Ribbons These are available in a wide variety of colours, materials, patterns and textures. Ribbons can be used functionally as drawstrings or as decoration.

Sewing threads These are used to machine-stitch fabrics together or to embellish designs.

Trimmings Many different kinds are available, from simple braids to highly decorative pom-poms and fringing.

Wool threads (yarn) Tapestry wool thread is a strong matt embroidery thread that works very well on woollen fabrics; use a large-eyed tapestry needle. Knitting wool can also be used for embroidery or to make your own pom-poms.

Key

1 Beads and buttons	5 Wool thread (yarn)
2 Embroidery threads (floss)	6 Binding tape
3 Fabrics	7 Ribbon
4 Sewing threads	8 Felt
	9 Trimming

EQUIPMENT

Very little specialist equipment is needed for appliqué work. The most important item is a sharp pair of scissors. Keep scissors used for cutting fabrics and threads separate from those used for paper and cardboard, otherwise they will quickly become blunt.

Beading needle This needle is specially designed for stitching beads on to fabric. It is very fine and flexible, and particularly useful for tiny beads.

Dressmaker's pins These are used to pin fabrics together before tacking (basting) and stitching. Do not use blunt or rusty pins as they will leave holes or marks in the fabric.

Dressmaker's scissors These should be used for cutting fabric only. Do not use them to cut paper or cardboard, as this will blunt the edges.

Embroidery scissors These small scissors are very sharp, and are used to trim fabrics and cut threads. Do not use them to cut large areas of fabric.

Fading fabric felt-tipped pen This pen is very useful for drawing designs on to fabric. The marks will fade on contact with air or water (see Basic Techniques).

Iron Always check the temperature before ironing different fabrics. If possible, it is a good idea to use a separate iron for iron-on fusible bonding web.

Sewing machine A sewing machine with different stitch settings can be used for appliqué. Bobbins can be filled with a different coloured thread from the top thread to create decorative effects. Hand-sewing then can be used for decorative finishes.

Needle threader This is not essential, but does help when threading hand-sewing needles.

Pinking shears These specialist scissors have serrated blades, designed to cut fabrics so that the edges do not fray. They should not be used to cut paper.

Quilting pins These are longer than standard dressmaker's pins and can pin several layers of fabric and wadding (batting) together.

Pencil A pencil is useful for scaling up templates. To mark fabrics, use one of the materials listed here.

Ruler Use a metal ruler to draw straight lines on fabric. You may also need a ruler to enlarge the size of a template.

Safety pins These can be used to hold layers of fabric together. A safety pin is also needed to thread a drawstring through a fabric casing.

Tailor's chalk This is particularly useful to mark dark shades of fabric or those with uneven texture. It will rub off or disappear after washing.

Tape measure This is more flexible than a ruler and is also used to measure lengths of fabric.

Key
1 Pinking shears
2 Tape measure
3 Sewing machine
4 Quilting pins
5 Embroidery scissors
6 Bobbins
7 Needles
8 Needle threader

BASIC TECHNIQUES

The basic idea behind appliqué is a very simple one: small pieces of fabric are applied to a background fabric to create decorative effects. However, the following techniques will make the task easier and will aid in the success of the final result.

TRANSFERRING ORIGINAL DESIGNS

Tracing Templates
1 Place a piece of tracing paper over the chosen shape. Draw round the shape, using a soft pencil.

2 Remove the tracing paper and turn it over. Scribble over the drawn lines as shown. Turn the tracing paper over again and place it on a piece of paper or thin card (stock). Draw over the original drawing.

3 The shape should now be transferred to the paper or thin card. Go over it with a pencil if it is faint. Cut out the template.

Enlarging Templates
To enlarge a template, trace it on to graph paper following the above instructions. Decide the scale you want to enlarge it to then draw it again on a piece of larger-size graph paper. You can also enlarge templates on a photocopier.

Using a Fabric Felt-tipped Pen
This is used to draw round a template to transfer the shape on to fabric. The marks made by a fading fabric pen gradually disappear on contact with air or water. You can also use a dressmaker's pencil.

Using Tailor's Chalk
This is useful for drawing designs on dark fabric or fabrics with an uneven texture. The chalk marks wash out or rub off.

IRON-ON FUSIBLE BONDING WEB

1 Set an iron to medium heat. Iron the bonding web on to the reverse side of the fabric.

2 Place the template on the backing paper of the bonding web. Draw round the shape, using a pencil, then cut out carefully with a pair of scissors.

3 Remove the backing paper. Position the shape on the background fabric and iron it in place.

SATIN STITCH APPLIQUÉ

1 Draw the shape you wish to appliqué on a piece of fabric. Pin this on to the background fabric. Machine-stitch round the outline with straight stitch.

2 Using a sharp pair of scissors, trim the excess appliqué fabric, cutting close to the machine stitches.

3 Machine-stitch over the first stitched outline and the edge of the shape, using satin stitch or an embroidery stitch.

TACKING (BASTING) ON TO PAPER

1 Draw round the template on to a piece of fabric. Cut out, allowing an extra 5mm (¼in) seam allowance as shown.

2 Cut another paper template and place it on the back of the fabric shape. Tack (baste) the seam allowance over the edge of the paper, gently pulling the thread. Snip the fabric at points (for example, the inner point of a heart design) to help it fold over neatly.

3 Using a hot iron, iron over the back. Carefully remove the tacking stitches and the paper template.

4 Pin the appliqué shape on to the background fabric. Hand- or machine-stitch round the edge.

REVERSE APPLIQUÉ

1 Draw round the template on to the main fabric. Draw another line about 5mm (¼in) inside the shape. Using sharp scissors, cut out the inner shape. Clip the 5mm (¼in) border at intervals then fold back to give a smooth outline. Press in place with a hot iron.

2 Place a contrasting fabric behind the outline shape and pin. Stitch round the edge of the shape.

CUTTING AND FOLDING EDGES

Curves

1 Using a sharp pair of scissors, snip into the dip in the curve up to the marked line. For the outside of the curve, cut out evenly spaced triangular notches of fabric.

2 Fold over the edge along the marked line to the wrong side. Press with a hot iron then tack in place.

Points

1 To make a neat folded point, cut away the fabric around the point as shown.

2 Fold over the edge along the marked line to the wrong side. Press with a hot iron then tack in place.

Inside Angles

1 At the inner point of the angle, snip the fabric up to the marked line.

2 Fold over the edge along the marked line to the wrong side. Press with a hot iron then tack in place.

HAND STITCHES

Many different embroidery stitches can be used to attach and embellish appliqué shapes. These are some of the most commonly used hand stitches.

Stab Stitch

Bring the needle through to the right side of the fabric. Start as close to or as far from the edge as you wish, depending on the size stitch required. Insert the needle into the background fabric to make a straight stitch.

French Knots

Bring the needle through the edge of the shape to the right side of the fabric. Holding the thread taut with your left hand, twist it several times around the needle. Still holding the thread taut, turn the needle and insert it back through the fabric at the same point. Pull gently on the needle to form a neat knot.

Feather Stitch

Starting at a point of the appliqué shape, bring the needle through the edge to the right side of the fabric. Make slanting stitches alternately to left and right, pulling the needle through the loop in the thread with each stitch. The stitches on the left will hold the shape in place.

Blanket Stitch

Work from left to right. Bring the needle through the appliqué shape to the right side of the fabric. Start as close to or as far from the edge as you wish, depending on whether you want a small or large stitch. Work a vertical stitch, catching the thread under the tip of the needle as you draw it through the fabric. Space the stitches as evenly as possible.

Running Stitch

This is the simplest hand appliqué stitch. Bring the needle through the edge of the appliqué shape to the right side of the fabric. Insert the needle back in the fabric, leaving a gap about the same size as the stitch. The stitches can be any size. You can alternate the length of the stitches for decorative effect.

Cross stitch

Bring the needle through the appliqué shape to the right side of the fabric. Start as close to or as far from the edge as you wish, depending on whether you want a small or large stitch. Insert the needle in the background fabric at an angle. Bring the needle out again on the appliqué shape immediately above this point. Make a stitch in the opposite direction to the first to form a cross.

HEART GIFT DECORATIONS

It is always such a treat to receive a handmade card and matching gift box. It doesn't take a huge amount of time but the result is so special. The designs in this particular project are rich and sumptuous in their colours and fabrics, which make them perfect for Valentine's Day but you could easily adapt the idea to suit other special occasions using different shades and motifs.

1 Cut out small hearts from scraps of organza, slightly smaller than the width of the organza ribbon. You will need about 20 hearts per metre (yard) length of ribbon.

2 Sew each heart on to the ribbon with running stitch and a contrasting thread that will show up against the fabric. Alternate the colours of the hearts along the length of the ribbon.

3 For the gift tag, cut a piece of coloured thin card to the size required and punch a hole at the top.

▶

Materials and Equipment You Will Need
Dressmaker's scissors • Scraps of organza fabrics • 1cm (³⁄₈in) wide organza ribbon • Needle and contrasting sewing threads • Paper scissors • Coloured thin card (stock) • Hole punch • Embroidery threads (floss) • Double-sided tape • Decorative cord • Ruler • Assorted beads • Small gift box

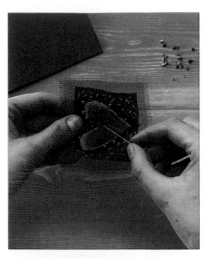

4 Cut out a heart from organza and lay it on a square in a contrasting colour. Lay a third piece of organza over the top. Decorate with stitches using embroidery threads and tape to the tag.

6 For the greetings card, cut a piece of thin card 12 x 20cm (4 x 5in) and fold in half. Use layers of organza to make up the main design, tacking (basting) the fabric together to hold in place.

7 Embellish the appliqué with decorative beads and stitches. Fix the appliqué design to the card with double-sided tape as before.

5 Cut a length of decorative cord and thread it through the punched hole. Tie the two ends in a knot.

8 For the gift box, assemble another appliqué design, using a combination of fabrics, and tacking them in place as before. Embellish with beads and decorative stitches and fix to the lid with tape.

KITCHEN COLLAGE

Blue and white plain and patterned fabrics make a very attractive fabric collage to hang on the wall of a kitchen or breakfast room. Display the picture as it is, as a small wall hanging, or mount it in a box frame so that the glass does not touch the appliqué. The collage would also work well in shades of another colour such as pink or green, to match your china.

1 Cut two pieces of striped and plain fabric for the background to make an overall size of 34 x 42cm (13½ x 16½in). Machine-stitch together then cover the join with fabric tape. Fold under the edges by 1cm (½in) and press. Pin in place.

2 Iron fusible bonding web on to the reverse side of scraps of plain and patterned fabrics.

3 Trace the coffee pot and cup shapes from the back of the book and make templates (see Basic Techniques). Draw round the templates on to the bonding web and cut out.

Materials and Equipment You Will Need
Dressmaker's scissors • Striped and plain cotton fabrics • Sewing machine and matching threads • Fabric tape • Iron • Dressmaker's pins •
Iron-on fusible bonding web • Scraps of plain and patterned fabrics • Tracing paper • Soft pencil • Paper or thin card (stock) • Paper scissors •
Fading fabric felt-tipped pen • Embroidery scissors • Needle • Embroidery threads (floss) • Small pom-pom (optional) • Buttons •
Pom-pom trimming • Craft (utility) knife • Mounting (mat) board • Double-sided tape

4 Peel off the backing paper from the coffee pot shapes and position on them the fabric background. Iron in place. Repeat steps 1–4 for the coffee cup.

6 Work a swirl in running stitch on the top of the cup to indicate steam. Stitch a wavy line of running stitches to indicate steam coming out of the spout of the coffee pot.

7 Stitch the pom-pom trimming along the bottom edge of the picture, as shown, so that the pom-poms show on the right side of the design. ▶

5 Decorate the appliqué with simple stitches. Outline some of the shapes with stab stitch or blanket stitch to accentuate them against the background. Sew a small pom-pom or button on the lid of the coffee pot.

Simple decorative hand stitches complement the country-style design.

8 Hand-stitch neatly around the folded edges of the picture.

10 To frame the appliqué, cut a piece of mounting board large enough to leave a wide border all around the picture. Attach the appliqué with a strip of double-sided tape along the top edge. Sign the picture in pencil, if you like.

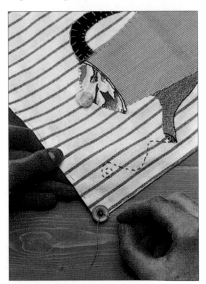

9 Sew a decorative button at each corner.

ALPHABET APRON

Large, bold shapes and bright colours are ideal for this child's apron. The cotton fabrics are strongly stitched with double seams and zigzag stitching, so the apron will stand up to plenty of wear and frequent washing.

1 Fold the main fabrics in half widthways. Wrong sides facing and matching centre points, pin together along one side. Machine-stitch, fold over the seam and stitch again. Mark curves at the top corners as shown and cut. Hem the edges.

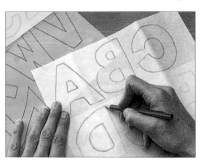

2 Enlarge the letters from the back of the book to 7cm (2¾in) high (see Basic Techniques). Reverse and make templates.

3 Draw round the letters on to the backing of the fusible bonding web. Iron the bonding web on to the reverse of scraps of fabric, using different colours for adjacent letters, and cut out.

4 Arrange the letters neatly in five rows on the apron fabrics. Peel off the backing paper and iron in place once you are happy with the arrangement.

5 Using matching threads, zigzag-stitch round the edges of the letters.

6 Cut the tape or ribbon for the ties into four equal lengths. Machine-stitch to the top sides of the apron and either side of the neck edge. Knot the neck ties together and adjust to fit. Gently hand-wash the apron as required and carefully iron once dry.

Materials and Equipment You Will Need
40 x 70cm (16 x 28in) red cotton fabric • 30 x 40cm (12 x 16in) blue cotton fabric • Dressmaker's pins • Sewing machine and matching threads • Tailor's chalk • Dressmaker's scissors • Tracing paper • Soft pencil • Graph paper • Paper or thin card (stock) • Paper scissors • Iron-on fusible bonding web • Iron • Scraps of cotton fabrics, in bright colours • Embroidery scissors • 1.5m (60in) of 2cm (¾in) wide yellow fabric tape or ribbon

HANDS AND HEARTS THROW

Use your own hand as the template for this traditional quilted throw. The symbolic motifs and check cotton fabrics are borrowed from American folk designs, generating a feeling of warmth and hospitality. In this project, the buttons are not simply for decoration; they serve to quilt the layers of fabric together. Lay the throw out flat for quilting and work from the centre outward.

1 Draw round your hand in pencil. Draw round the outline again in felt-tipped pen, simplifying the shape.

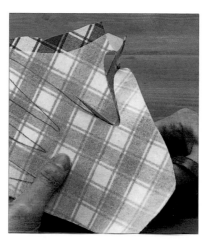

2 Trace the hand shape and transfer it on to the paper side of the fusible bonding web (see Basic Techniques). Iron the bonding web on to the reverse of a piece of check fabric and cut out.

3 Draw a heart shape on to bonding web. Iron the bonding web on to the reverse of a piece of contrasting fabric and cut out. Iron the heart on to the hand as shown.

▶

Materials and Equipment You Will Need

Soft pencil • Paper • Felt-tipped pen • Tracing paper • Iron-on fusible bonding web • Dressmaker's scissors • Iron • Scraps of check cotton fabrics, in different colours • 1.5m (60in) square of heavy cream cotton fabric • Dressmaker's pins • Sewing machine and matching threads • 1.6m (64in) square of check cotton fabric, for the backing • 1.5m (60in) square of polyester wadding (batting) • Safety pins • Stranded cotton embroidery threads (floss) • Needle • Assorted buttons

4 Make 11 more hand shapes, varying the fabrics. Iron a heart shape on to each hand, as in step 3. Peel off the backing paper.

5 Position the hands on the cream fabric, leaving a border of about 25cm (10in) all round. Pin in place then iron.

6 Using matching threads, machine-stitch around both the hand and the heart shapes in a close zigzag stitch.

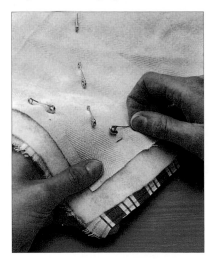

7 Lay the backing fabric out flat, with the wrong side facing upward. Centre the wadding on top. Lay the appliqué right side up on top. Trim the wadding so that the backing fabric is 6cm (2½in) larger all round. Secure the three layers together with safety pins.

8 Press under 1cm (½in) of the backing fabric all round. Fold over to the right side of the throw and press under 5cm (2in) to make a border. Pin, then machine-stitch, mitring the corners. Using six strands of embroidery thread, sew buttons between the hand shapes.

The secret to working with different patterns is to choose a limited range of colours.

ANGEL STOCKING

Different shades of dark blue and faded denim work very well together, showing that you do not always need to use bright or contrasting colours in appliqué. This is a good way to recycle old jeans and denim shirts. Make the Christmas stocking as large or as small as you wish – the denim fabric is certainly strong enough to carry the weight of plenty of presents!

3 Decorate the angel with different embroidery stitches, as shown. Stitch the features on the face and the hair.

1 Trace the angel shapes at the back of the book and make templates (see Basic Techniques). Iron fusible bonding web on to the back of scraps of denim. Draw round the templates on to the bonding web and cut out.

2 Draw a large stocking shape on a piece of paper and cut out to make a template. Draw round the template on to two pieces of denim and cut out. Remove the backing paper from the bonding web. Position the appliqué shapes on the right side of one stocking piece and iron it in place.

4 Sew buttons around the angel and scattered over the rest of the stocking. ▶

Materials and Equipment You Will Need

Tracing paper • Soft pencil • Paper or thin card (stock) • Paper scissors • Iron • Iron-on fusible bonding web • Scraps of denim, in different shades • Dressmaker's pencil or fading fabric felt-tipped pen • Dressmaker's scissors • Needle • Embroidery threads (floss) • Buttons • Dressmaker's pins • Ribbon • Sewing machine and matching threads • Pinking shears • Gingham fabric

5 Right sides facing, pin the two stocking pieces together, leaving the top edge open. Cut a 12cm (4¾in) length of ribbon, fold in half and trap between the two stocking pieces on one side, about 6cm (2½in) below the top. Machine-stitch the pieces, leaving a 1cm (½in) seam. Neaten the raw edges with pinking shears.

7 Place the denim stocking inside the lining stocking, matching the top raw edges. Pin the denim and lining together around the top opening. Machine-stitch, leaving a 1cm (½in) seam.

6 For the lining, use pinking shears to cut two stocking shapes from gingham fabric. Right sides facing, pin together, leaving the top edge open. Machine-stitch, leaving a 1cm (½in) seam and a 15cm (6in) gap along one side.

8 Push the denim stocking through the gap in the lining then push the lining inside the denim stocking. Slip-stitch the gap. Stitch a line of running stitch around the top edge of the stocking. Make up additional stockings in the same way, varying the designs.

TOY BAG

Tidy away toys or laundry in this strong cotton drill bag. The appliqué dog motif is made of different scraps of left-over fabrics, ironed in place with fusible bonding web. If you want to use the toy bag for wet washing or sports clothes, you can make a plastic lining to go inside the bag.

1 Right sides facing, fold the cotton drill fabric in half widthways. Machine-stitch the side seams, stopping 25cm (10in) from the top. Reverse-stitch to reinforce the stitching. Fold back the top edges by 10cm (4in) so that the right sides are facing. Stitch, leaving a 1cm (½in) seam allowance, and fold right side out. Turn the bag right side out.

2 To make the casings for the ribbon ties, cut two strips of contrasting fabric. Fold these in half lengthways and press with an iron. Open out then fold the sides into the centre. Fold over each end. Position one on each side of the bag and stitch in place leaving open at one end. Cut a second piece of contrasting fabric measuring 23 x 21cm (9 x 8¼in). Fold under 6mm (¼in) on each side and press.

3 Trace the dog shapes from the back of the book and make templates (see Basic Techniques). Iron the fusible bonding web on to the reverse side of scraps of different fabrics. Draw round the templates on to the bonding web and cut out. Position the dog shapes on the fabric panel and iron in place.

4 Stitch on a bead for the dog's eye and embroider French knots for the nose. Stitch a button on the collar.

5 Position the panel on one side of the bag and pin in place. Machine-stitch. Stitch a button to each corner by hand.

6 Cut the ribbon in half. Fasten a safety pin to one end then thread one through the casing. Secure at either end with pins. Thread the second ribbon through the other casing and pin the ends. Cut each felt square into two triangles. Trap each pair of ribbon ends between two triangles then stitch all around the edge in running stitch.

Materials and Equipment You Will Need
Dressmaker's scissors • 50 x 150cm (20 x 60in) cotton drill fabric, for the bag • Sewing machine and matching threads • Two plain, contrasting fabrics • Iron • Tracing paper • Soft pencil • Paper or thin card (stock) • Paper scissors • Iron-on fusible bonding web • Scraps of different fabrics • Needle and embroidery threads (floss) • Embroidery scissors • Bead • Buttons • Dressmaker's pins • 3m (3yd) narrow ribbon • Safety pins • Two 10cm (4in) squares of felt, in different colours

8 Stitch some of the shapes on to the blanket, using stab stitch (see Basic Techniques) and a contrasting wool.

10 Fill in the background with individual large cross stitches.

9 Stitch the remaining shapes on to the blanket, using blanket stitch.

Stab stitch is decorative and holds the appliqué shape in place.

MOSAIC VELVET CUSHION

This rich velvet cushion cover is a clever way to use scraps of fabric. The triangular shapes and decorative embroidery are reminiscent of crazy patchwork, which was very popular in the Victorian era. The aim at the time was to create a random design, hence the name. To create a mosaic effect, the pieces may be arranged more regularly. To make up the cushion, see the Inlaid Boat Cushion project.

1 Measure the cushion pad. For the cushion front, cut a piece of velvet to this size plus 2cm (¾in) all round. Cut triangles in different sizes from scraps of contrasting velvet. Press under the edges of the triangles by 7mm (⅜in), ensuring that the edges are straight.

2 Trim the excess fabric at the corners. Tack (baste) around the edge of each triangle. Arrange the triangles on the background velvet and pin in place.

3 Slip-stitch neatly round the edge of each triangle. Remove the tacking (basting) stitches.

4 Outline some of the triangles with feather stitch, using contrasting embroidery threads.

5 Stitch round the edge of other triangles with blanket stitch and other decorative embroidery stitches. Make up the cushion and insert the pad.

Materials and Equipment You Will Need

Tape measure • Cushion pad • Dressmaker's scissors • Velvet • Scraps of contrasting velvet • Iron • Embroidery scissors • Needle • Tacking (basting) thread • Dressmaker's pins • Matching sewing threads • Embroidery threads (floss)

COUNTRY CANDLESHADES

Natural-coloured linen and textured appliqué fabrics complement one another to create these charming candleshades. Fray the edges of the fabrics and decorate the design with pearl buttons and embroidery stitches to complete the effect. In this project, the template is used in the finished candleshade to back the appliqué. Do not leave the candleshades unattended at any time when in use.

1 Enlarge the candleshade shape from the back of the book so that it measures 10cm (4in) high (see Basic Techniques). Transfer on to thin card and cut out to make a template.

2 Using a fabric felt-tipped pen, draw round the template on to the linen fabric. Cut out the fabric, adding an extra 1.5cm (⅝in) for turnings.

3 Draw small hearts on scraps of fabric and cut out. Cut small squares of fabric and fray the edges slightly. Appliqué some of the heart shapes through the squares on to the candleshade fabric, using stab stitch and two strands of embroidery thread.

4 Add the single heart shapes. Sew pearl buttons in the middle of some of the appliqué hearts and scattered over the background. Vary the stitches used.

5 Place the appliquéd shade face down on a protected surface and spray lightly with adhesive. Place the card template on top. Fold the edges of the linen to the inside, smoothing the fabric as you go.

6 Fold in the raw edge and glue lightly. Bend the candleshade into shape and hold together with paper clips until the glue is dry. Slip-stitch the joined edge if necessary, stitching through the card.

Materials and Equipment You Will Need

Tracing paper • Soft pencil • Graph paper • Thin card (stock) • Paper scissors • Fading fabric felt-tipped pen • 25 x 35cm (10 x 14in) natural-coloured linen • Dressmaker's scissors • Scraps of natural-coloured and textured fabrics • Embroidery scissors • Needle • Stranded cotton embroidery threads (floss) • Small pearl buttons • Craft adhesive spray • Fabric glue • Paper clips (fasteners)

CHRISTMAS TREE STARS

Red and green, the traditional festive colours, are mixed and matched in these two complementary designs. Both are simple and quick to make by hand, using small, neat running stitches. As an alternative to this bold, coordinated effect, you can experiment with a variety of different colours or embellish the Christmas decorations with beads, sequins and shiny threads.

1 Draw a star shape on to paper or thin card and make a template. Using tailor's chalk, draw round the template on to felt.

2 Cut equal numbers of red and green stars from the felt.

3 Using the point of the scissors, pierce one of the red stars 5mm (¼in) from the edge. Cut out a smaller star, leaving a 5mm (¼in) border all round. ▶

Materials and Equipment You Will Need

Soft pencil • Paper or thin card (stock) • Paper scissors • Tailor's chalk • Red and green felt • Embroidery scissors • Needle and matching threads • Scraps of patterned fabric • Ribbon

4 Stitch the red border to one of the green stars with small, even running stitches and matching thread.

5 Centre a small red star cut out in step 3 on a green star. Stitch in place.

6 Place the stars from steps 4 and 5 together, sandwiching a plain red star in the middle. Stitch the three stars together at the inner points, as shown.

7 For a different decoration, take a green felt star and cut a small circle from the centre. Place on top of a red star, with a small piece of patterned fabric showing through the hole. Stitch neatly round the hole in running stitch.

8 Stitch the two stars together around the edges with stab stitch.

9 Use a loop of ribbon for hanging. Alternatively, wrap sewing thread around all four fingers. Stitch a loop on to a point of each star with small stitches.

INLAID BOAT CUSHION

Inlaid appliqué is a variation on the basic technique in which the design is drawn on the background fabric and cut out, leaving open spaces. The cut-out shapes are then placed on fabrics in contrasting colours, cut out again and the contrasting colours are used to fill the spaces. This technique is best suited to fabrics of the same thickness which do not fray, such as blanket and heavy woollen fabrics.

1 Trace the templates from the back of the book and enlarge to the size required (see Basic Techniques). Measure the cushion pad and cut out a piece of blanket fabric to this size plus 2cm (¾in) all round. Position the templates on the main fabric. Using a fabric felt-tipped pen, draw round the templates on the reverse of the fabric.

2 Using a sharp pair of scissors, cut out the shapes from the main fabric.

3 Place each cut-out shape on a piece of different-coloured blanket fabric, pin and cut out. ▶

Materials and Equipment You Will Need

Tracing paper • Soft pencil • Paper or thin card (stock) • Paper scissors • Tape measure • Square cushion pad • Dressmaker's scissors • Blanket fabrics in different colours • Fading fabric felt-tipped pen • Dressmaker's pins • Embroidery scissors • Contrasting cotton fabrics for the back • Fabric glue and brush • Tapestry needle • Wool threads (yarn) • Needle and sewing thread • Scrap of felt • Cord • Large button • Beads • Narrow ribbon • Iron • Sewing machine • Four pom-poms

4 Cut a piece of cotton fabric larger than the boat design. Glue on to the back of the piece in step 1, behind the cut-out areas.

5 Place the coloured cut-out shapes in the openings and pin in place. Using coloured wool threads, hand-stitch the shapes to the surrounding blanket with large stab stitches.

6 Use coloured wool threads to decorate the sails with French knots (see Basic Techniques) and an appliqué star cut from a scrap of felt.

7 Cut a small fabric rectangle for the cabin and appliqué in place as shown. Using sewing thread, stitch on a piece of cord for the mast, add a large button at the top, then sew a bead to the bottom corner of each sail. Stitch ribbon across the boat's hull, using cross stitch.

8 To line the design, cut a piece of cotton fabric the same size as the cushion front and place it on the reverse of the appliqué. For the cushion back, cut two pieces of fabric in different colours, to the width of the front but two-thirds of the length. Fold under and press a 1cm (½in) double hem on both opening edges; machine-stitch. Right sides facing, place the cushion front on the two overlapping back pieces and machine-stitch all round. Turn the cushion cover right side out. Hand-stitch a pom-pom to each corner.

SHADOW-APPLIQUÉ SCARF

This delicate, floaty scarf is made of layers of chiffon, with squares of fabric appliquéd at random with a leaf-like motif. Chiffon is rather a slippery fabric so it is best to tack the layers securely together before machine stitching. The raw edges of the appliqué are finished with decorative embroidery stitches, and the edges of the scarf are rolled and stitched by hand.

1 Cut a piece of chiffon 30 x 105cm (12 x 41½in). Press in half lengthways, open out then press folds 15cm (6in) along length. Cut 17cm (6¾in) squares of chiffon. Tack (baste) one square to the reverse of the main piece, using fold lines as a guide.

2 Following the fold lines, machine-stitch the square in place. Trim the excess fabric 3mm (⅛in) outside the stitch line. Repeat along the scarf.

3 Make a leaf and circle template. Using a fabric felt-tipped pen, draw round the templates several times on to different squares of chiffon.

4 Pin each appliqué square on to a contrasting square on the scarf, choosing squares at random. Tack in place, then machine-stitch around the shape. Trim the excess fabric 3mm (⅛in) outside the stitch line.

5 Using doubled sewing thread, stitch along all the machine-stitched lines in feather stitch to cover the raw edges.

6 Using your forefinger and thumb, carefully roll each edge of the scarf until the raw edges are concealed. Stitch in place with slip stitch.

Materials and Equipment You Will Need
Dressmaker's scissors • Chiffon, in three different colours • Iron • Dressmaker's pins • Needle • Tacking (basting) thread • Sewing machine and matching threads • Soft pencil • Paper or thin card (stock) • Paper scissors • Fading fabric felt-tipped pen • Embroidery scissors

HEART-WARMING HATS

Brighten up a cold winter's day with these cheerful appliqué hearts and flowers, stitched on to two ready-made woollen hats and a scarf. Decorate the simple shapes with beads, buttons and embroidery threads (floss), using oddments from your needlework box. Use a cool iron for woollen fabrics and take care not to stretch or distort them when you stitch on the appliqué shapes.

1 For the button heart hat, draw a large heart shape on paper or card and cut out to make a template. Draw round the template on to a piece of fusible bonding web. Iron on to a piece of felt and cut out.

2 Position the heart on the front of the hat. Iron in place, using a cool iron.

3 Using embroidery thread in a contrasting colour, stitch around the edge of the heart in stab stitch.

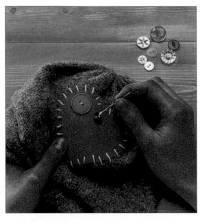

4 Decorate the heart with buttons in different sizes and colours.

Materials and Equipment You Will Need
Pencil • Paper or thin card (stock) • Paper scissors • Iron-on fusible bonding web • Embroidery scissors • Iron • Scraps of felt • Woollen hats • Needle • Embroidery threads (floss) • Various buttons, in different sizes and colours • Fading fabric felt-tipped pen • Woollen scarf • Beading needle • Small glass beads • Knitting wool (yarn) • String

5 For the flowery scarf, draw two flower shapes on to paper or thin card and cut out. Using a fabric felt-tipped pen, draw round both templates on to scraps of felt.

6 Position the flowers at either end of the scarf. Using embroidery threads, attach with a few stitches in the centre of each flower.

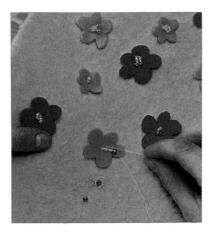

7 Thread a beading needle and knot the end of the thread. Thread on a few beads and stitch down in the centre of a flower. Decorate all the flowers in the same way.

8 Stitch short lengths of embroidery thread in the spaces between the flowers, using a single running stitch. Tie the ends in a double knot then trim.

9 For the heart hat with pom-pom, draw two heart shapes on to paper or card, one smaller than the other. Cut out to make templates. Iron fusible bonding web on to scraps of felt. Draw round the templates several times on to the bonding web and cut out. Place the larger heart shapes round the edge of the hat and iron in place, then place smaller hearts on top and iron in place.

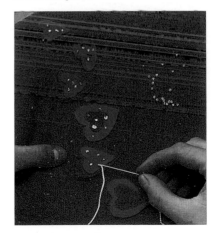

10 Decorate the hearts with stitches and beads, using embroidery threads in contrasting colours. ▶

11 To make the pom-pom, cut two 12cm (4¾in) diameter circles in card. Cut out a 4cm (1½in) diameter circle from the centre of each. Place the two together and wrap knitting wool around them and through the hole until the central hole is filled. Insert the blades of a sharp pair of scissors between the two pieces of card and cut the wool. Pass a piece of string between the two pieces of card and knot. Remove the card circles.

12 Fluff up the pom-pom to make a ball and trim. Stitch to the top of the hat.

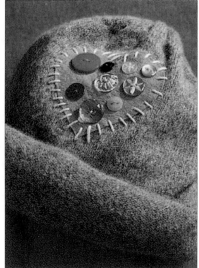

A heart embellished with buttons makes a contemporary decoration.

SPOTTED CUSHION

The different textures of towelling, velvet and wool come together in this appliqué cushion. The circles are cut out and then filled in with different fabrics from behind, using the reverse appliqué technique (see Basic Techniques). The stitching is done by machine, except for the pom-pom edging. If you cannot find a trimming in a suitable colour, try dyeing one with fabric dye.

1 Measure the cushion pad and cut a piece of woollen fabric to this size plus 2cm (¾in) all round. Using tailor's chalk, draw round a circular object on to six squares of the same fabric, as shown.

2 Position the squares on the large piece of woollen fabric, not too close to the edge. Pin in place.

3 Machine-stitch round each circle in a straight stitch. Remove the pins.

4 Using sharp scissors, cut through both layers of fabric inside each circle close to the stitching. Push the rest of the fabric through the hole and press in place. Cut out squares of velvet and towelling in different colours, larger than the holes. Pin a fabric square behind each hole then machine-stitch round the edge of the circle.

5 To make the cushion back, cut two pieces of fabric in different colours, to the width of the front and two-thirds of the length. Use pinking shears if desired. Fold under and press a 1cm (½in) double hem on both opening edges. Machine-stitch. Right sides facing, place the cushion front on the two overlapping back pieces and stitch all round.

6 Turn right side out. Hand-stitch the trimming round the edge. Insert the pad.

Materials and Equipment You Will Need

Tape measure • Cushion pad • Dressmaker's scissors • Woollen fabric • Tailor's chalk • Circular template • Dressmaker's pins • Sewing machine and matching threads • Embroidery scissors • Iron • Scraps of velvet and towelling, in different colours • Two fabrics in different colours, for the back • Pinking shears (optional) • Pom-pom trimming • Needle and matching thread

GARDENER'S APRON

Modern technology and traditional craft meet in this striking design, which makes use of a heat-transfer machine at a photocopying store. You can use other images in magazines or photographs to create your own personalized apron, perhaps for a cook or artist. You can use image-transfer gel instead of the heat-transfer machine in step 2. Allow the prints to cool and dry before folding or moving them.

1 Cut a selection of flower images out of magazines and photographs. Glue them lightly on to the A4 paper.

3 Using a cool iron, iron fusible bonding web on to the reverse of the bespoke flower print fabric.

4 Cut out the flower shapes and arrange on the apron. Peel off the backing paper and iron in place, using a cool iron and a piece of cotton fabric.

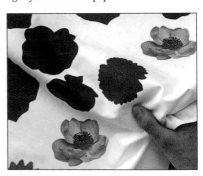

2 Take the chosen cotton fabric to a photocopying store with a heat-transfer machine. Transfer the images to the fabric. Leave to cool.

5 Stitch around the outline of each flower, using stab stitch and matching sewing threads.

Materials and Equipment You Will Need
Paper scissors • Flower images from magazines or photographs • Paper glue • Sheet of A4 paper • White cotton fabric • Iron • Iron-on fusible bonding web • Embroidery scissors • Apron • Needle • Matching sewing threads

FELT CURTAIN

This bold abstract design can brighten a window or be used to disguise an untidy corner. Machine-stitched stripes are overlaid with colourful circles, attached with large hand stitches. The felt fabrics will not fray so there is no need to worry about finishing the edges of any of the shapes. Make the curtain to fit the area desired; a larger version would make a good room divider.

1 Measure the blue felt and cut to the size of curtain required. Cut the cream felt into strips 4cm (1½in) wide then pin on to the blue felt 4cm (1½in) apart. Using blue thread, machine-stitch down each side.

2 To make hanging loops, cut a piece of blue felt 12cm (4¾in) wide and the width of the curtain. Using some tailor's chalk, mark every 4cm (1½in). Cut down each marked line to the last then cut out every alternate bar. Leaving a 4cm (1½in) band, cut the bottom.

3 Thread a needle and tack (baste) the inlaid pieces securely in place. ▶

Materials and Equipment You Will Need
Tape measure • Blue felt • Dressmaker's scissors • Metal ruler • Cream felt • Dressmaker's pins • Sewing machine and matching threads • Tailor's chalk • Embroidery scissors • Scraps of coloured felt • Cutting compass and mat (optional) • Needle • Embroidery threads (floss)

4 Lower the feed on the sewing machine and attach a darning foot. Either place the piece in a wooden embroidery hoop or hold the fabric firmly between your fingers. Stitch a wobbly line around the outlines of the dog and kite shapes in a contrasting woollen thread, using the same thread in both the bobbin and on the top. On each snowflake, stitch a star shape in a contrasting thread.

5 Draw the kite tail freehand with a fabric felt-tipped pen, and stitch it.

6 Unfold the piece and pin the two side edges together with the right sides facing. Raise the feed on the sewing machine and attach a presser foot. Stitch the seam, leaving a 2cm (¾in) seam allowance. Refold the piece with the seam line at the centre back.

7 Fold the embroidered section to the right side. Pin and machine-stitch a seam across the top edge of the inside section.

8 To make fabric ties, cut two strips of wool fabric 5 x 25cm (2 x 10in). Fold the strips in half lengthways and tuck in and pin a narrow seam allowance. Work a wide zigzag stitch over the long edge and one short edge.

BRODERIE PERSE TABLECLOTH

The idea of cutting motifs out of printed fabrics and appliquéing them on to plain fabric can be seen in early quilts. Imported chintz fabrics from the Far East were too highly prized to be thrown away after use, so the best portions were saved and recycled in this way. For the appliqué motifs, choose fabrics which do not fray or paint the edges with anti-fraying solution, available from specialist craft stores.

1 Fold the tablecloth into quarters and mark 25cm (10in) from the centre on each crease with a pin. Unfold the tablecloth. Using a tape measure and the pins as a guide, pin a 50cm (20in) square in the centre.

2 Use a pair of embroidery scissors to cut motifs from the printed fabric. The motifs can be cut out fairly roughly at this stage.

3 Iron fusible bonding web on to the reverse of the motifs. Cut them out carefully, as close to the outlines as possible. If necessary, treat the edges with anti-fraying solution. ▶

Materials and Equipment You Will Need
Plain tablecloth • Tape measure • Dressmaker's pins • Embroidery scissors • Printed fabric, with suitable motifs • Iron • Iron-on fusible bonding web • Anti-fraying solution (optional) • Thin card (stock) • Sewing machine and matching sewing threads • Napkins

4 Arrange some of the motifs along the inside edge of the marked square.

6 Using matching threads, machine-stitch around the edge of each motif with a close zigzag stitch.

5 Arrange the rest of the motifs within the marked square, in a more random pattern. Slip a piece of card under the tablecloth to protect your work surface. Peel off the backing paper and iron the motifs in place.

7 To make matching napkins, appliqué single motifs to the corners, using fusible bonding web and anti-fraying solution if necessary, as before. Hand-wash all of the items carefully as required.

APPLIQUÉ BED LINEN

Customized bed linen is simple to make and will give a real lift to bedroom decor. These designs can be added along borders or scattered across the main fabric – it all depends upon how adventurous you feel. The duvet cover uses a variation on the technique of cut-work appliqué, meaning that the design is cut out from the main fabric and a contrasting colour stitched underneath.

1 Draw star shapes on to paper or thin card and cut out. Draw round the stars on to scraps of coloured fabric using a vanishing fabric felt-tipped pen, allowing a 1cm (½in) seam allowance.

2 Cut out the fabric stars, snipping into the seam allowance up to the drawn outline as shown. Do not cut into the actual star shape.

3 With wrong sides facing, iron the seam allowance back on to the star to make neat edges.

Materials and Equipment You Will Need
Pencil • Paper or thin card (stock) • Paper scissors • Scraps of cotton fabric • Vanishing fabric felt-tipped pen • Dressmaker's scissors • Iron • Cotton pillowcase • Dressmaker's pins • Needle • Tacking (basting) thread • Sewing machine • Contrasting sewing threads • Duvet cover • Embroidery scissors

4 Position the stars along one edge of the pillowcase, pin and tack (baste) in place.

5 Select a contrasting colour and use a running stitch to machine-stitch the stars in place. Remove the tacking (basting) threads.

6 For the duvet cover, for each circular motif you will need to cut out two circles of fabric in contrasting colours.

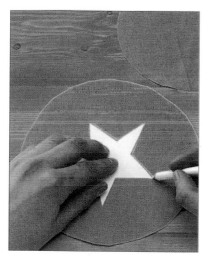

7 Using the star template from the pillowcase, draw round the star on to the wrong side of one of the fabric circles.

8 Use sharp embroidery scissors to cut out the star 5mm (¼in) in from the outline, leaving the circle intact. Snip into the seam allowances as before and, wrong sides facing, iron the seam allowance to form a neat edge.

9 Place the circle with the cut-out motif on top of the right side of the remaining circle, pin and tack in place. ▶

10 Machine-stitch round the edges of the star shapes and carefully remove the tacking threads.

12 Position the shapes on the duvet cover, pin and tack in place. Machine-stitch round the circles using plain and decorative stitches in contrasting colours. Remove the tacking stitches.

11 Snip round the circle, 1cm (½in) in from the edge, and press in place as before.

ORGANZA EVENING BAG

This exquisite little bag is decorated with delicate organza flowers, simply made of fringed and gathered bias strips. A single flower is stitched to the gold ribbon ties to neaten the ends. The bag is too beautiful to hide away in a drawer when not in use – fill it with pot pourri or herbs and hang it on a dressing table or bedpost. A larger bag could be made to hold a nightdress.

1 Draw an oval shape on paper, 14cm (5½in) long and 11cm (4¼in) at the widest point. Cut out, pin on to cream organza and cut round. Cut two pieces of blue organza 18cm (7in) wide and 20cm (8in) high.

2 Place the two pieces of blue organza together, fold in half and machine-stitch the short side. Right sides facing, tack (baste) to the cream organza oval then stitch. Turn the bag right side out.

3 To make the ribbon casing, fold over 1cm (½in) on the open edge and slip-stitch. Use transparent thread for all the hand stitching.

4 Cut 11 different-coloured organza strips on the bias, varying the width between 1.5cm (⅝in) and 3cm (1½in). ▶

Materials and Equipment You Will Need
Paper • Pencil • Tape measure or ruler • Paper scissors • Dressmaker's pins • Cream organza • Dressmaker's scissors • 40cm (16in) blue organza • Sewing machine and matching threads • Needle • Tacking (basting) thread • Transparent sewing thread • Scraps of contrasting organza • Safety pin • 50cm (20in) narrow gold ribbon

5 Fringe one side of each strip by pulling and rubbing the threads. Work a line of large running stitches along the other edge of each strip.

6 Pull the end of the thread to gather the organza, at the same time twisting the strip of organza around your finger to create a flower shape.

7 Stitch each flower at the base to secure the shape.

8 To make a fuller flower, place two flower shapes together, one inside another. Stitch together with small stitches at the base. Make another four flowers in the same way, mixing the colours. Leave one flower single.

9 Stitch the double flowers on to the bag, arranging them in a bouquet.

10 Fasten a safety pin to the end of the ribbon and thread it through the casing. Knot the ends then stitch the single flower to the knot.

ANGELIC BABYGROW

This outfit is guaranteed to make any baby look sweet and good! Position the wings on the upper part of the babygrow, about where the baby's shoulder blades will lie. The wings are lightly padded with a layer of wadding to give a slightly quilted effect when you machine-stitch the outlines. The same technique and design could be used to decorate other baby clothes.

1 Trace the wing shapes and make templates (see Basic Techniques). Using a fabric felt-tipped pen, draw around the top wing shape on to a piece of interfacing then iron on to the reverse of the blue fabric. Iron interfacing on to the reverse of the pink fabric.

2 Draw around the bottom wing shape on to the interfacing side of the pink fabric. Cut out both shapes, leaving extra blue fabric on the edge marked 'A', as shown. Repeat steps 1 and 2 for the other wing.

3 Tack (baste) the two parts of each wing together, making sure that the two pieces of interfacing butt together. ▶

Materials and Equipment You Will Need
Tracing paper • Soft pencil • Paper or thin card (stock) • Paper scissors • Fading fabric felt-tipped pen • Lightweight iron-on interfacing • Iron • Blue and pink jersey fabric • Embroidery scissors • Needle • Tacking (basting) thread • Lightweight wadding (batting) • Sewing machine and matching threads • Babygrow

4 Tack each angel wing on to a small piece of wadding.

6 Position the wings on the babygrow and tack in place. Slip-stitch in place, using matching threads.

5 Using blue thread machine-stitch around the edges of the wings, using a straight stitch. Cut away the excess wadding. Machine-stitch the decorative outlines. Set the machine to satin stitch and stitch round the edges of the wing.

RIBBON CUSHION

Collect different woven and brocade ribbons for this cushion, then machine-stitch them on to a ticking background, using the stripes as a guide. Always stitch from the top down to avoid puckering the ribbons. Complete the period effect with a braid border. If you only have short lengths of ribbon, make a small sleep pillow or herb bag and fill it with pot pourri or lavender.

1 Cut the ribbons into 35cm (14in) lengths. Arrange them to make a pleasing design.

2 Starting from the righthand side, machine-stitch the wide ribbons on to the ticking background with a close zigzag stitch. Follow the stripes to keep the ribbons straight.

3 Add the narrow ribbons, stitching them on top of the previous layer.

4 Measure the finished size of 33 x 53cm (13 x 21in) and mark with a fabric felt-tipped pen. If necessary, trim the ribbons to this size.

5 Stitch a narrow double hem along one edge of each 33cm (13in) square of fabric for the back opening. Right sides facing, pin one side to each short edge of the ribbon appliqué so that the trimmed edges face inwards. Stitch all round, leaving a 1cm (½in) seam. Turn the cushion cover right side out.

6 Starting at one corner, stitch the braid all round the cushion, using slip stitch. Gather the braid slightly at the corners. Conceal the join in the ends at the final corner. Insert the cushion pad.

Materials and Equipment You Will Need
Embroidery scissors • About 1m (1yd) each of ten ribbons, in different widths • Two 36 x 46cm (14 x 18in) ticking, with the stripes parallel to the short sides • Sewing machine and matching threads • Ruler • Fading fabric felt-tipped pen • Two 33cm (13in) squares of fabric, for the back • 155cm (61in) decorative braid • 30 x 40cm (12 x 16in) cushion pad

ROSE PETAL LAMPSHADE

Organza works particularly well used to decorate a plain lampshade, with the light intensifying the delicate colours. The petal shapes are applied in layers to create a three-dimensional effect. Adjust the number of petals, depending on the size of the shade. Mix toning colours such as reds and pinks or purples and lilacs. Use a low wattage bulb and do not leave the lamp unattended.

1 Draw two petal shapes on paper, one larger than the other. Using the large template, cut out about 20 petals in different shades of organza.

2 Cut out about 20 small petals, using the smaller template.

3 Using a paintbrush, glue a row of large petals 5cm (2in) above the bottom edge of the shade, alternating the colours. Apply the glue only at the pointed end of each petal. Overlap the petals as shown to cover the shade.

4 Gradually work up the shade to the top, mixing large and small petals and varying the colours. Leave to dry.

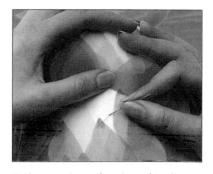

5 Alternatively, stitch each petal in place, using transparent thread. Try not to stitch through the whole shade but only into the silk or cotton surface.

6 Using a small amount of PVA glue or a needle and some transparent thread, fix the trimming round the top of the shade. Fold the trimming to the inside and glue or stitch in place.

Materials and Equipment You Will Need

Pencil • Paper • Paper scissors • Dressmaker's pins • 40 x 40cm (16 x 16in) each of three toning shades of silk organza • Dressmaker's scissors • Small paintbrush • PVA (white) glue • Saucer • Silk or cotton lampshade • Needle • Transparent sewing thread • Lampshade trimming

LACE CUSHION

Natural linen fabric and scraps of heavy white lace combine beautifully in this small cushion, finished with pearl beads and a fringed edge. Use several different styles of guipure lace to make the design interesting. The same idea would work equally well on a dressing gown or drawstring bag. To prevent the edges of the lace motifs from fraying, paint on an anti-fraying solution.

1 Draw a large letter, 12cm (4¾in) high, on paper and cut out to make a template. Draw round the template on to the right side of one linen square. Cut out lace motifs, choosing shapes that will fit the shape of the letter.

2 Treat the lace edges with anti-fraying solution. Leave to dry. Transfer the motifs to the linen and tack (baste) in place.

3 Using white sewing thread, stitch the motifs in place with small stab stitches. Wrong sides facing, hand- or machine-stitch the two squares of linen together, 3cm (1½in) from the edge, leaving a 5cm (2in) gap along one side. Pull away threads for 2cm (¾in) to fringe the edges. Fill with a small amount of wadding. Slip-stitch the gap.

4 Stitch the narrow lace edging along the stitch line, to cover the stitches and decorate the edges.

5 Using a beading needle, stitch tiny pearl beads to the centre of the flower-shaped lace motifs. Stitch a daisy motif to each corner of the cushion.

Materials and Equipment You Will Need

Pencil • Paper • Paper scissors • Fading fabric felt-tipped pen • Two 22cm (8½in) squares of heavyweight natural-coloured linen • Embroidery scissors • Scraps of white guipure lace, including scroll and flower motifs • Anti-fraying solution • Needle • Tacking (basting) thread • Sewing machine (optional) • White sewing thread • Wadding (batting) • 90cm (35½in) narrow white lace edging • Beading needle • Tiny pearl beads

FELTED APPLIQUÉ ORGANZA

In this beautiful translucent piece the design is made using wool fibres, which are sandwiched between layers of net and organza and then felted together. Felting is quite a messy process so make sure you have plenty of space to work in. Use the finished piece as a curtain or room divider.

1 Cut the lengths of organza and net in half. Place one piece of organza on top of one piece of net.

3 Place more layers of wool horizontally on top. Then place a third layer vertically over the top. If desired, add silk fibre to the wool fibre.

4 Trim the edges of each mound of wool, shaping them into squares or rectangles.

2 Pull out a thin layer of wool fibre 5cm (2in) long. Lay the wool vertically on the organza. Repeat to make a design.

5 Repeat the vertical and horizontal layering process all around the edges of the organza, to create a woollen border, as shown.

Materials and Equipment You Will Need
Dressmaker's scissors • 3.2m (3½yd) white silk organza • 3.2m (3½yd) plastic net • 750g (2lb) white merino wool fibre •
25g (1oz) silk fibre (optional) • Needle and matching thread • Large plastic sheet • Dishwashing detergent • Iron

6 Place the other pieces of net on top of the design.

7 Hand stitch the two pieces of net and organza together all around the edge with large stitches.

8 Protect the work surface with a sheet of plastic then wet the fabric 'sandwich' with some water.

9 Apply dishwashing detergent over the fabric, to help the felting process.

10 Roll up the fabric along one edge. Start to felt it by rubbing the surface gently with your hands in a circular movement for a few minutes, then unroll the fabric.

11 Continue rolling and felting each side for about 15 minutes. Wash the fabric thoroughly with warm water, open out flat and leave to dry. ▶

12 Remove the top layer of net and iron the felted fabric carefully on a very low heat setting.

14 The loops may be used to hang the fabric from a wooden frame to make a screen, or to hang from a window or corner of a room.

13 Securely stitch loops of thread on to each corner.

SEASIDE CHAIR

Transform a plain director's chair with a bold design of multicoloured flags flying from yellow sandcastles. The repeat motifs are fused on to the removable chair back with iron-on bonding web, then machine-stitched in place. Hand-embroidered French knots add an extra jaunty flourish. Work out how many sandcastles will fit on the chair back and space them evenly.

1 Iron the fusible bonding web on to the reverse side of the yellow fabric and on to the fabrics for the flags.

2 Trace the sandcastle and flag shapes from the back of the book on to paper or thin card to make templates and cut out (see Basic Techniques). Using a soft pencil, draw round the templates on to the bonding web. Cut out.

3 Remove the back from the chair. Peel off the backing paper from each shape and position on the right side of the chair back, as shown, with a flag above each sandcastle turret. Iron in place.

4 Machine-stitch round the edge of each shape with a close zigzag stitch. For the flagpoles, stitch a line of straight stitch to join the flags to the turrets.

5 Stitch a star on each sandcastle. Using embroidery thread, work a French knot at the top of each flag.

6 Cut a piece of fabric to cover the appliqué design, allowing an extra 5mm (¼in) seam. Turn under the seam and pin in place over the back of the appliqué, with wrong sides together. Slip-stitch in place.

Materials and Equipment You Will Need

Iron • Iron-on fusible bonding web • Yellow fabric, for the sandcastles • Scraps of different-coloured fabrics, for the flags • Tracing paper • Soft pencil • Paper or thin card (stock) • Paper scissors • Dressmaker's scissors • Director's chair • Iron • Sewing machine and matching threads • Needle • Soft cotton embroidery threads (floss) • Contrasting fabric, to line the chair back • Dressmaker's pins

TEMPLATES

If the templates need to be enlarged, either use a grid system or a photocopier. For the grid system, trace the template and draw a grid of evenly spaced squares over your tracing. To scale up, draw a large grid on to another piece of paper. Copy the outline on to the second square, taking each square individually and drawing the relevant part of the outline in the larger square. Finally, draw over the lines to make sure they are continuous. Alternatively, two different sizes of graph paper may be used.

SEASIDE CHAIR PP92–3

COUNTRY CANDLESHADES PP48–9

INLAID BOAT CUSHION PP53–5

ALPHABET APRON PP32–3

KITCHEN COLLAGE PP28–31

ANGELIC BABYGROW PP79–81

HEARTS AND STARS BLANKET PP42–5

TOY BAG PP40–1

ANGEL STOCKING PP37–9

INDEX